FENG SHUI
ANSWERS

"When you wish to contract something,
     You must momentarily expand it ;
When you wish to reject something,
     You must momentarily join with it ;"

Lao Tzu 80(36)

FENG SHUI
A N S W E R S

Vijayalakshmi Minocha

**Harnessing ancient Chinese wisdom to
Tap your true Wealth, Health and Success Potential**

Srishti
PUBLISHERS & DISTRIBUTORS

SRISHTI PUBLISHERS & DISTRIBUTORS
64-A, Adhchini
Sri Aurobindo Marg
New Delhi 110 017

Copyright © Vijayalakshmi Minocha 2000

Copyright © SRISHTI PUBLISHERS & DISTRIBUTORS 2000
First published in 2000 by Srishti Publishers & Distributors

ISBN 81-87075-57-0
Rs. 149.00

Cover Design by Vijayalakshmi Minocha

Printed and bound in India by
Saurabh Print-O-Pack, Noida

I dedicate this book
to the memory of my
Venerable Grandfather,
Shri. Vasudevendra Saraswati Swamigal

"Human beings are,
     soft and supple when alive,
     stiff and straight when dead.
Therefore, it is said:
     The rigid person is a disciple of death:
     The soft, supple, and delicate are lovers of life.
The unyielding and mighty shall be brought low:
The soft, supple, and delicate will be set above."

Lao Tzu 41(76)

COMMENTS

DENISE LINN is an internationally acclaimed lecturer, author and healer.
She originated the practice of *"Interior Alignment"*
and is the author of the best-seller-
"Sacred Space Clearing and enhancing the energy of your Home",
among several other widely recognized books, video & audio cassettes on
transforming one's inner and outer space. Denise is on the faculty of the
Metropolitan Institute of Interior Design in New York and is a member of the
Board of Advisors of the Feng Shui Guild. Every year thousands of participants
attend Denise's Space Clearing seminars throughout the world.
Her comments on this book, very briefly, are:

"It is exciting to me that you are writing about Feng shui from a
perspective of one of the most ancient cultures on earth".
"It focuses mostly on the Compass school,
but is reaching out to a broad market."
"Your comparison of Vaastu Shastra to Chinese Feng shui is absolutely the
best comparison I have ever read, and it made me hungry to read your book
on the subject when it comes out.
I think the Feng shui world will embrace that book."
"I am privileged to have been able to see your newest offering to the
heavens &/send you may support and love for your journey in Life"

FOREWORD

Feng Shui is an ancient Chinese art dating back to at least 220 BC. Some theorize, that perhaps it is much older. The parallel Indian practice of Vaastu also dates back a very long time. Apart from a few missionary works in the late nineteenth century, the first English books on Feng shui date from my *Living Earth Manual of Feng Shui* written in 1976.
Vijayalakshmi has now made Feng shui accessible to readers in India, a country whose people already understand the necessity of building and orientating homes in a way, which will bring maximum blessings to the occupants.

Why has the spread of Feng shui taken so long?
China has a long history of giving up its arcane secrets very slowly. Other examples could be quoted such as kung fu which only reached the western world properly in the last half of the 20th century. The secret of gunpowder manufacture, too, was successfully kept a secret by the Chinese for hundreds of years, much before it changed the face of war in Europe.

Feng Shui is one of the more complex Chinese sciences to have been exported, and even now a lot of the more detailed practices of Feng shui are still only available in Chinese.

Fortunately Vijayalakshmi tackles Feng shui in a refreshingly no nonsense manner, with clear and helpful diagrams. The book is structured as a series of questions and answers and it covers the questions most frequently asked about Feng shui.

From the vast mailbag of queries we regularly get about Feng shui at *Feng Shui for Modern Living*, magazine, I can certainly confirm that she has covered many of the key issues.

I wish her, and her readers, every success in the practice of one of the most ancient arts which addresses many of our most modern problems.

Stephen Skinner
Founder and Publisher of Feng Shui for Modern Living

CONTENTS

ACKNOWLEDGEMENTS

My Feng shui voyage has had its first stepping-stone with this book.

I am thankful to my publishers for helping to crystallize my maiden foray.

I am also grateful to ….

My Family-a mountain of support---- always compensating and nurturing.

My Esoteric Idols & Shining Stars of the Feng shui world ---

Stephen Skinner, Raymond Lo, Lillian Too, Jami Lin & Denise Linn ;

All of whose blessings, I humbly solicit.

Ankur, at my office, for his painstaking efforts.

Anju and Vijay for their timely and immaculate artwork.

My little daughter, who is, undoubtedly

The revitalizing "*Sheng Ch'i*" of my life & work.

PREFACE

Q. Who all is this book meant for?

A. Through this book, I want to reach out to

- Most of you, who are hard-pressed for time and need some bite-sized, practical ideas on how to improve your life in every way.
- Those of you, who need some basic, simply written, easy- to- understand, point-wise clarity on Feng shui.
- Some of you, who have a very hazy notion of Feng shui and are curious to learn about its "*why's*" and "*how's*".
- All the persons, who are informed to some extent, but have scores of doubts regarding the usage, validity, and effectiveness of Feng shui.

"FENG SHUI ANSWERS" attempts to bring the incredible wealth of Feng shui wisdom "Out of the Closet," so-to-speak, and into each one of your lives; help you overcome all difficulties with ease and realize abundance, at the wake of the new millennium.

Q. What are the skills and benefits I can get from this book ?

A. A Brief summary of what you will get from this book:

- Professional and certified answers to *all* your queries ever about Feng shui. You need look no further for an introduction to Feng shui, one that would appeal to the most die-hard logical skeptic.
- *Where* and *how* to begin the process of improving the atmosphere and luck of your own house with Feng shui.
- The various things to watch out for in Feng shui Malpractice.
- To what extent you can simply and practically implement Feng shui "*cures*"- like wind chimes, crystals etc.

This vital guide cuts through the esoteric jargon right to the crux of the issue. FENG SHUI ANSWERS provides an easy way for anyone to all about Feng shui in the shortest possible reading time.

The Question and Answer format helps in getting across **focused ideas**; miniaturized and quality information at your finger tips. Prospective users of Feng shui may realize what all they really would need to know in order to reap maximum benefits of its usage.

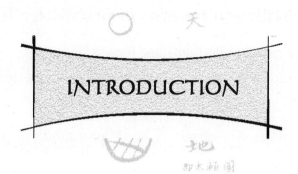

INTRODUCTION

FENG SHUI (pronounced "Fung Shway") is the ancient Chinese art of attuning to our environment, the cycles of nature, unseen earth-forces and planetary vibrations. It has been used effectively over the centuries to bring good tidings, health and prosperity. This book, (the first in a series), is a means to share with you this unique wisdom of our ancestors. **It assists you in aligning yourself to your space so as to realize incredible abundance in your current lifespan.**

Before giving out the *ANSWERS*, let me ask *YOU* some questions:

- Do you wonder, how some people just have it going for them all the time, in spite of very similar set-ups?
- Would you like to change the flow of your fortunes, without spending much time and money?
- Do you think Feng shui is just a lot of New-Age hogwash with no scientific basis?

1

- Don't you want to know the real story behind the huge popularity of Feng shui?
- Is your house lucky for you and your family? Can you make it *more auspicious*?
- Can you enhance the success of your relationships/marriage?
- Is there any hidden reason in your surroundings for any frequent accidents, losses or illnesses?
- Can you protect your house from undesirable elements/events while at the same time making it a tranquil and refreshing place?
- Do you mind having more Joy, Success and Prosperity-all without losing your Peace of Mind?

I urge you to read on with an open mind and heart, so that, you too can join the thousands of others who have woken up to the rather surprising benefits of using a little Feng shui in their Life & Space.

Vijayalakshmi
New Delhi
1999

ESSENTIAL MEANING & RELEVANCE

Q. What is Feng shui ?

A. "FENG SHUI", (literally translated " Wind" "Water" in Chinese), is a time-honored system of rules, concepts and principles that explains how our lives are inextricably linked to the way of the universe. It is a system by which you can get your surrounding space to do more than just the apparent function. **Feng shui makes your living and work area nourish & nurture you.** It can be very unobtrusively applied to any space, structuring it symbolically to bring in greater wealth, success, and happiness into your life.

It is a collection of universal facts that asserts, that, by just aligning your furniture, accessories to your beneficial energy lines you can overcome many of life's difficulties. Good Feng shui prevents bad things from happening to you and your family, in addition to unblocking a veritable ocean of abundance, which is rightfully yours.

> **Feng shui is a Chinese philosophy , which expands on how the arrangement of an environment affects the Life & Luck of people, inhabiting it.**

Q. What does Feng Shui affect ?

A. Feng shui affects every aspect of your life. It provides valuable guidelines for each spatial act of yours, from- how you place your dining table/ bed/ sofas to what colour of front door/ upholstery is most auspicious for you. It **emphasizes the** need to work with the energies that surround us, than to be oblivious and indifferent to them. Most importantly, **it assists you in circumventing difficulties in your path and emerge a Winner in all aspects of life- career, family, education etc.**

Q. What is Feng Shui used for ?

A. This science/art is seen as a definite way to significantly improve health, fortune, and happiness by stimulating the right energies and aligning your bodies with the space we inhabit and work in. It is used for unblocking the hidden potential in your environment.

The greatest utility of Feng shui lies in its uncanny knack of setting things right in your life—simply by creating inner accord in the *"soul"* of your outer space.

People all over the world have successfully used different degrees of Feng shui to infuse positive energy in all what they do, and several times alleviate some very frustrating problems. An amazing " coincidence" that most people find hard to grasp at the start, is the direct and powerful link between the way each part of their home is oriented/ arranged and their aspirations/ difficulties. This 3000-year-old art has some eminently practical formulae that even any laypersons can use to their advantage.

The **Do-it- yourself appeal** of Feng shui is perhaps what makes it useful to all kinds of people with or without much resources to get professional help.

> There is a Direct and Powerful Link between the way
> Each Part of your Home is Oriented / Arranged
> and your Aspirations / Difficulties

Q. Who can benefit from Feng Shui ? Can you name some people ?

A. Each and every one of you can. Beneficiaries include several of the world's biggest power lords, industrialists, Hollywood stars etc. all of whom have used Feng shui modifications in their home and work place to help them get that rich and famous. Some of these, people are - Donald Trump, Richard Branson, Gillian Anderson, Anita Roddick of Body Shop, Hong Kong tycoon Li Ka-shing. Companies include British Airways, Hutchinson Telecom and several Fortune 500 companies who have branch offices, units in South East Asia.

The native Chinese businesses and tycoons are in any case steadfast followers and beneficiaries of Feng shui.

Q. What do people generally look to Feng Shui for ?

A. People across the world, look to Feng shui **for answers, to the typical tribulations of life**. These include- **Souring relationships, children's repeated failure to do well in studies, constant monetary losses, Family tension and stagnating jobs.** Several persons hire Feng shui experts to make detailed analyses of their properties and suggest areas for improvement.

Feng shui offers them **ways to realize a lot of their aspirations** that they just wish for, but feel one lifetime is not enough. All persons who have been touched by Feng shui in some form or the other, have always come back for further consultation and incorporate suitable adjustments on a regular basis, to always keep their home or office working best for them.

A lot of corporate houses and Business Firms keep Feng shui consultants on the rolls to keep the **synergy** in their organization. Young entrepreneurs benefit from having their office *"done- up"* with auspicious arrangements and symbols of wealth and success.

The symbols of Feng shui-like the *"Pa-Kua"* mirror, Wind Chimes, Auspicious calligraphies, good luck talismans are all immensely popular as they are very powerful in effect, and you don't need to get any detailed evaluation to be able to avail their benefits. (Plate no.12)

Q. The promises made seem rather improbable. How can Feng shui alter my destiny ?

A. The potency of Feng shui, and the extent of how much you benefit from using its principles stem from your **"Trinity of Luck"** - Heaven Luck, Man Luck, Earth Luck.

- "Destiny" is Heaven Luck (**Time**)-according to the Chinese. This affects about 40% of our lives and is unchangeable.
- "Man Luck" (**Action**)- roughly around 25%, is how you take care of your physical, mental, emotional, spiritual health.
- "Earth Luck" (**Space**)-- is the awareness of your energetic status and conscious efforts at harnessing Universal energy. This last 35% is left solely in our hands to maximize or diminish.

Now, as you can see, your destiny, in reality just controls less than half of your fortunes. The rest is all your own doing. Feng shui consciousness can greatly promote your chances for a fulfilled, happy and healthy life.

> ### Your Destiny,
> ### in reality just controls Less than Half of your Fortunes.
> ### The Rest is all Your Own Doing....

Q. How come Feng shui is so popular, especially in the west ?

A. It is easy to see that westerners are very prompt in capitalizing on any way of getting wealthier. They have a lot of enterprise and their economy is built up with venture capitalism as a hallmark. Eastern cultures are recently coming into the limelight with the **promise of abundance through personal development**. Many western companies with Hong Kong subsidiaries practice Feng shui including Citibank and Shell. Even those who are quite skeptical at the start, submit eventually to the enveloping influence that good Feng shui positioning brings to their organizations. In several cases, the practice of Feng shui is also taken into their homes. The western mindset readily adopts the sound wisdom of Feng shui, once the initial doubt is replaced with actual proof of its amazing benefits.

Q. What are the historical origins of Feng shui ?

A. The earliest known records of Feng shui originate from the Southwest region of China during the *Han* Dynasty (206B.C-220A.D). The mountainous *topography* inspired a philosophy for finding beneficial location for dwellings and burial sites. The resultant "*Form- School*" Of Feng shui as this came to be known was refined further in A.D 888 by the teachings and practice of *Yang Yun Sung*, who was at the time, an advisor to the Emperor. The plains of Southeast China on the other hand did not have a similar landscape. So another approach called the "Compass School" of Feng shui was developed during the *Song* Dynasty around 1000 A.D.

The astrological aspects of Feng shui had core inputs from India and Tibet.

Q. How can I learn more about Feng shui ?

A. From several books available commonly in all bookstores. Also by attending courses mostly in the U.K, U.S, conducted by leading Feng shui *"Sifu"* (Master-Teacher). One good way to get a practical feel of Feng shui is to get a professional to give your home and / or office a once over. This would give you a little insight into how profound life changes via Feng shui actually work. Such an experience will impart realism to your efforts, animating your bookish knowledge immediately.

"Act before there is a Problem;
Bring Order before there is Disorder"

Lao Tzu 27(64)

Q. Would I be able to practice Feng shui after reading few books on the subject ?

A. To a limited extent. This is because, there is more to Feng shui than just Placement. Reading a few works may give you a surface understanding of the fundamental principles and basic theories. This is all at best only *half* of what Feng shui is all about.

The other, important part is the *Art.* The more challenging part, which requires a deep understanding of the concepts, their comparative analysis and layered application in real life situations. This is possible only by attending courses under renowned masters and by contemplating intensely on all available reading material.

Laypersons can apply Feng shui to their own situation, on the basis of tips and advice gleaned from books. The only thing is that the degree of the change is generally proportional to the depth of working knowledge.

"Harmony implies Constancy ;
Constancy requires insight.."

Lao Tzu 8(55)

Q. What is so special about Feng shui versus any other placement technique ?

A. Feng shui offers, in addition, a vital starting point for realizing our dreams, strengthening our health and grounding our intuition in a pragmatic manner. It is **a very personalized and proactive art of placement, with solutions totally**

conforming to **Modern Living**, with its attendant space & time- crunch, technological dependence and fluctuating socio-economic structure.

Q. How can a science formulated in ancient times, assist our modern lifestyle ?

A. As I have mentioned earlier, Feng shui is very constructive and practical in its approach to all the accouterments and fixings of modern living. Gadgets or appliances that can make your life a little easier are all working towards a similar goal-greater happiness to you.

Modern Living is fraught with new and varied kinds of stresses. One thing that can really help us all is a relaxing and refreshing home atmosphere. This is in each of our hands to achieve... *Feng shui can show us the way.*

> **Feng shui offers solutions totally conforming to Modern Living**

Q. Isn't Feng shui mostly applicable to Chinese people ?

A. Chinese society is one that pays a lot of emphasis on obedience, respect for elders and harmonious relationships in a family unit. These are considered to be far more important than wealth. They firmly believe prosperity can be self-destructive without an overall balance in life. This is probably what really sets them apart in the quiet manner in which they **accumulate wealth, without the incredible opulence affecting their family structure and code of ethics**.

Feng shui opens a window into how this is possible- how can one get seriously rich, stay rich, and yet be completely relaxed, at peace with oneself and have a harmonious family life. The essence of Feng shui is that **inner happiness is the basis for all round prosperity,** and not the other way around as is commonly believed.

Therefore, I would say that Feng shui is particularly appropriate, only to the Non- Chinese who have a lot to gain from its profound wisdom.

Q. Is the ancient Indian *"Vaastu Shastra"* any more effective than Feng shui, for determining auspicious locations ?

A. *"Vaastu Shastra"* is often erroneously referred to as *"Vedic-* Feng shui". It is a parallel, equally "grounded" placement Science, but much older. It is **based on insightful observations made about the relation between Solar Radiation and House Form.** Its recommendations are based on the precept that Human Beings are affected in a uniform set of ways by all the unseen forces of nature. It has laid down a complex set of guidelines for organizing all forms of activities in the most auspicious locations, among several other rules for living the most harmonious life. There is an underlying Spiritual consciousness, which was considered an indispensable part of Vedic Life.

Feng shui on the other hand treats each person according to **his/her unique astrological make-up and lays down 8 categories of people**. Each of these is allocated 4 auspicious directions and 4 inauspicious directions. Besides this, there are several other contextual considerations for determining the most appropriate location for any purpose.

Therefore, as you can see, **each of these systems is valid**. But, they are products of entirely different socio-cultural groups with radically varied cosmologies and world- views. *Their theories are mutually exclusive as well as inclusive.* **It takes a person with an acute grasp and thorough knowledge of both sciences to practice a correct combination of both, without misinterpreting either.**

THE CONCEPT OF
YIN AND YANG

THE COMPLEMENTARY YET
ANTAGONISTIC ELEMENTS IN NATURE

A balance of these elements is essential for harmony and success.
The concept of Yin and Yang is the bedrock upon which
Most oriental philosophies are supported;

The grasp of which is indispensable for any valid
spatial analysis done from the Feng shui point of view.
A list of commonly understood Yin and Yang elements
is given in Plate no. 2

The key to its application is being able to identify the
Yin / Yang category of each element in your surroundings.

Plate No. 1

IMPORTANT FEATURES & CLARIFICATIONS

Q. Does Feng shui work ?

A. Definitely. You may have experienced some days when you are totally out of sorts, with nothing going right. This is an example of a conflict in your energy equation with your surroundings. Some times this can be quite detrimental, when it starts affecting your physical, mental or emotional health. Here is exactly where Feng shui comes in....*to figure out what are the main causes in your home that need certain adjustments.*

Feng shui thus gets the complex world of cosmic forces that manipulate our fortunes and happiness into the practical realm of interior design. It offers very personalized, simple solutions that really do get results when correctly implemented. Thousands of people across the world have experienced a **complete lifting of the stresses and stagnant luck in their lives, greater clarity and all kind of wonderful opportunities opening up to them, after getting some Feng shui assistance.**

Q. How exactly does it work ?

A. The central unit of Feng shui philosophy is the omnipresent life-force called _"Ch'i"_, in Chinese. This is a vital energy that animates everything on earth. When it is flowing well and is in abundance, the environment flourishes. Conversely, when _Ch'i_ level is low, its flow blocked, people in that environment tend to be listless, and overcome with frustrations.

Feng shui works by manipulating and directing this life force. It asserts that, by understanding and accessing the flow of this _Ch'i_, individuals can create a happier life full of abundance for themselves and their loved ones. By subtly making your home a more beautiful and nurturing haven for you, Feng shui uplifts your state of mind; As when we you feel well and energetic, your actions and thoughts are more focused. This brings about radical and often very surprising results in terms of opening out of opportunities, overcoming persistent health problem etc.

Q. Do I have to believe in Feng shui for it to work for me ?

A. The practice of Feng shui does **not** require either faith or fervent belief. Nor does it require the compromise of any of your religious convictions or personal values. You may not realize a space has been touched by Feng shui unless you allow yourself to _Feel_ the positive atmosphere of the place and see how the occupants have suddenly had things going there way. Your own commitment to lead a more fulfilling life is all that is needed.

Feng shui is just a collection of universal facts. So believing in Feng shui is similar to believing in, say, the weather. The point is that the only belief you need is that a large part of your **"destiny"** is in your own hands. The house that supports you can assist you in amazing ways to realize your aspirations, if only you structure it in the most auspicious manner.

Q. What kind of results can I expect ?

A. After suitable Feng shui additions and /or alterations have been made:

- The space feels a great deal lighter and livelier.
- You will experience a pronounced clearness of mind, along with the ability to perform your work with greater ease.

These are just the instant sensations of an enhanced space. **The real benefits lie at a deeper, subconscious level from where the harmonious vibrations will start to flow.**

- Your relationships to people around you will improve, and,
- You will experience fulfillment in all your endeavors.

Q. Does it involve any superstition, magic or dangerous practices ?

A. Not at all. Most Feng shui practices are based on common sense, rational judgment, scientific and astrological correlations and natures way -all these with a touch of mysticism. But it is certainly not any type of magic or supernatural jugglery. It is sensible, down-to-earth aesthetics for the body and soul of your home and workplace.

In ancient China it was not uncommon for Feng shui to be infused with superstition, but most modern day Feng shui has relegated supestition to the past and is very practical.

Also, there is also absolutely NO danger in any manner of Feng shui application. It is only concerned with human welfare in all spheres of life. The only danger is, that of *missing out* on your full potential in life, if you do not incorporate Feng shui in clearing your energetic paths and realize a stress free abundant life.

Q. Does Zen philosophy have anything to do with Feng shui

A. Zen as a philosophy is simply everyday life lived with extra awareness and quiet contemplation. Feng shui philosophy is about enhancing day-to-day life too. So, if you can do your Feng shui, "*in a Zen way*", you would probably get much more satisfaction. The effects of the change brought on would be deeper and last longer.

Q. Is Feng shui connected with any religion?

A. Feng shui has its roots in ancient Chinese Society, which in turn was deeply influenced by *Ruist* and *Taoist* Philosophy. As such, the way Feng shui is structured for contemporary usage; there are NO religious connections. The suggestions are secular, with the right balance between the Scientific, The Intuitive and The Spiritual.

> **Feng shui is just a collection of Facts,
> about the energies around us.**
>
> **It has Nothing to do with Any Religion or Faith system**

Q. Is Feng shui only applicable to houses ?

A. Feng shui can be applied to all and every part of the built environment. This includes housing complexes, apartment blocks, offices,

factories, shops, showrooms, parks, public buildings, schools, hospitals etc...The beauty is that you can use Feng shui to energize even just your desk at work or any part of any space individually. It shares the monotheistic *Vedic* philosophic belief that the smallest creation on earth is a microcosm in itself, reflecting all the dynamic forces at it's own scale of existence. Thus **any space can be considered for Feng shui assessment and improvement**, not only houses.

Q. Do Feng shui changes require much money to be spent?

A. Sure, it is. Most Feng Shui can be done without any expense (for example, moving a chair out of the way of a door so that it opens freely, etc.), but, there will be times when you might want to make a Feng shui investment that will have great rewards. In esoteric matters, which concern our fortunes and well being, we tend to be *unclear* about what our expenses are getting us in Real terms.

The study of relevant books on Feng Shui would also help you immensely in identifying the **genuine obstacles** in your surroundings that are impeding your personal progress.

Q. Will it affect my whole family?

A. The effects of Feng shui are not limited to the person who has initiated the consultation and effected the changes. His or her family of course immediately feels the harmonious vibrations, and receives the specific benefit/s.

Every person who even just enters such a *"Feng shui-ed"* space will notice a difference. Those who are more sensitive may comment on it, others may just feel more relaxed. The life- force-*Ch'i*, which is manipulated in Feng shui, feeds each person's energetic body mind and spirit.

Therefore; incorporating Feng shui in your home is like having a *Reiki* healing session on your home. In Reiki each part of the "healee" takes the required amount of the universal nurturing energy to become better.

In Feng shui a similar thing happens, with **each component, animate or inanimate of your home absorbing the requisite *Ch'i* to blend in better. This results in all members of your family including pets to be in harmony with the living environment of your house.**

> The key is to
> identify Genuine obstacles in your surroundings
> that are impeding your personal progress;
> And protect yourself against making wrong , potentially
> harmful adjustments to your home and/ or workplace

Q. If I do only a little change, would it still work ?

A. Yes, to a certain degree. The least you should do is to identify the possible impediments in your home to the optimum *Ch'i* flow. Then the smallest enhancement can make an enormous difference. Even if you are not able to do a reconnaissance of you home and randomly place an enhancement like a wind chime, a crystal or an auspicious calligraphy you may get very good results- providing you are clear about why you are purchasing a certain Feng shui item and where exactly it would work best for you.

Q. What is the guarantee that I will see a difference ?

A. All people are different in their destinies and what they make out of their Gift of Life. This art of Feng shui is over 3000 years old, tried and tested successfully by thousands of people around the world. Your own intention to do something about improving your life and space is itself a guarantee that thing are going to go your way.

A LIST OF COMMONLY UNDERSTOOD
YIN AND YANG ELEMENTS / ACTIVITIES

YIN	YANG
Earth	Heaven
Night	Day
Shadow side	Sunlit Side
Intuitive outlook	Scientific Outlook
Autumn/ Winter	Spring/ Summer
Even numbers	Odd Numbers
Graveyards, Hospitals	Electric substations,
Police Stations	Schools
Small windows	Large Glazing
Water Features	Plants, Flowers
Muted, cool colours	Bright, cheerful
colours	
Passive activities-	Active pursuits-
Reading, listening to music,	Swimming, Tennis,
Yoga	Dancing

Plate No. 2

Feng shui is just *one way to* make a difference in your health, wealth status—one that is the very popular, accepted, effective and versatile. A good Feng shui practitioner can very specifically design solutions/enhancements for your peculiar context. This analysis can guarantee fabulous results; just as the medication prescribed by a good, homeopath who looks at your problem **holistically.**

> ## Feng shui offers you Clues in your Environment to life problems of many kinds.
>
> - Your child/s disinterest in studies
> - Being accident and/ or illness prone
> - Constant monetary losses and setbacks
> - Stagnating career and frustrations in business
> - Frequent disappointments in love

Q. Can I actually get more *fortunate* with Feng shui ?

A. Activating good Feng shui involves energizing the excellent Chi flows that create and generate good luck. According to Feng shui, good fortune comes in many different guises. **Commonly, fortunes are in the form of wealth accumulation, in the form of recognition and fame, or in promotion to positions of power, status, and authority. Good fortune can also mean enjoying marital bliss, being blessed with a wonderful family, having loving and respectful**

children, and generally being able to enjoy easy, happy relationships with the people around you. Having vibrant good health, living to a ripe old age, or having the ability to concentrate effectively and thus acquiring useful skills or knowledge. Feng shui offers guidelines and, in some instances, specific measures that you can adopt for activating any or all of these different types of good luck in your life.

Q. How is this possible ?

A. By using both activating and counterbalancing Feng shui recommendations most suitable for you. Being both defensive and aggressive in your approach are simply two sides of the same coin.

For beginners, it is advisable to start by being defensive, thereby guarding yourself against bad Feng shui, before thinking about moving on to activate good luck.

Q. Will I need to knock walls or move doors for incorporating good Feng shui ?

A. Not necessary at all. The aim is to make some effort to achieve harmony and happiness, without causing undue duress.

It is generally quite difficult to disrupt any existing situation. Feng shui respects that, and can be interpreted for every level of intervention.

You may just want to add a small enhancement now, and take on changes gradually. That is a common way of proceeding with Feng shui adjustments. Some people, however, who are in the process of redoing or newly doing up their interiors, hire professional Feng shui consultants right from the start.

Obviously, *benefits are proportional to the extent and caliber of change made.* Even just minor alterations to the way you have arranged your drawing room seating, relocating the pot plants, adding a couple of decorative mirrors can beget you great abundance.

> ## Feng shui can be interpreted for Every level of intervention.
> ## Your Convenience is Paramount.

Q. How much of a lifestyle change is required for any Feng shui application ?

A. None! Quite simply, because, Feng shui IS about fitting in with your current lifestyle. The more you are in balance, the more powerful you become. So, incorporating Feng shui changes around the house brings you just that much more Peace of mind and a sense of well ness. And logically, the more you are in synchronicity with your surroundings, the more your house actually pays you back with good fortune and happiness

Q. How can the mere *position* of my furniture affect my life and fortunes ?

A. Replying this very commonly asked question is the sole purpose of many Feng shui books and articles.

Wrong furniture placement can-

- Block the flow of *Ch'i;*
- Create stagnation in some sphere of your life.
- Affect your energy levels by either adding to it or dissipating it.

Activities that receive an abundance of gently swirling *Ch'i*, generated by the objects placed correctly, flourish. Conversely with an absence of the life - giving "*Sheng-Ch'i*"(positive *Ch'i*), you may feel quite debilitated, your immunity goes down, and a gradual downfall in your fortunes can result.

Sharp edges of tables, chairs or open shelves send "*Shar- Ch'i*"(negative *Ch'i*) or poison arrows. Activities, people, spaces affected by these "arrows", suffer. (Plate no.10)

> Each House has its own "Climate"—
> A combination of
> air, light, scents, memories, colours....
> Furniture is a very important part of this "atmosphere".

Q. You mean, according to Feng shui, I cannot make any changes to, say, my décor, without affecting my luck ?

A. Feng shui does not entail the curtailing of your choices. It simply guides you in **going along with the flow rather than against it, by constantly struggling upstream**. It just offers you, personally auspicious choices of color, material, and texture for your design palette. (Plate no. 4)

Q. Can Feng shui work, if practiced incorrectly ?

A. No. Much of Feng shui demands good judgment and sensitive interpretation. Experience is certainly an important aspect of successful practice. Since it involves tampering to a great extent with the energies in your life, the caliber and grounding of the professional whose books you refer to is critical to what you can expect by following the given solutions.

You need to be extremely wary of "Closet- Practitioners"-especially in India, who perform erroneous and unprofessional Feng shui on you, in the guise of giving *"Vaastu"* or "Cosmic" advice.

Be wary of Unprofessional ,
"Closet- Practitioners" of Feng shui,
They peddle a Misleading and mostly Ambiguous
hodgepodge of "Cosmic" therapies,
allegedly…. for your "Well- being".

THE FIVE ELEMENTS
AND THEIR INTERACTIONS

These diagrams show the cyclical flow of Energy of the
Five Principal Elements of nature.

This figure shows that
Wood feeds on or produces Fire;
Fire produces Earth;
Earth produces metal;
Metal produces Water; and
back to Water that produces Wood

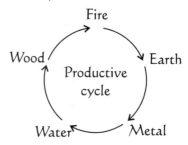

This figure shows that
Fire controls & destroys Metal;
Metal destroys Wood;
Wood destroys Earth;
Earth destroys Water
and finally Water destroys Fire

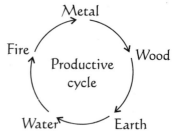

Understanding the dynamic relationships between these 2 cycles
enables Feng shui Practitioners to introduce individual balancing
elements in Homes and Work places.
This is done by either emphasizing or subduing specific elements.

Plate No. 3

Q. I hope Feng shui has nothing to do with the supernatural ?

A. No. It is firmly and solely for the living. Around 3000 years old,
Feng shui aims to tap into the earth's nurturing energy and harness it for creating environmental harmony.
It is interesting to note here that most Chinese Feng shui practitioners work with ghosts and house-spirits ... however modern western style Feng shui usually does not concern itself with the superatural.

Q. Is there any totally Feng shui designed building ?

A. Yes. There is a motel called *"MyHotel"*, a recently opened Boutique Hotel in London, U.K, which claims to be fully Feng shui attuned, and offer an oasis of calm and relaxation.

Q. How long does Feng shui take to work ?

A. The immediate changes are as described above, as the *Ch'i* starts to flow smoothly through the space and you. Subtler energetic changes that are more radical do take longer. The space and you take time to absorb the alignment. The greater the change desired, the longer it can take, but living a physically, emotionally and spiritually healthy life can get very speedy results.

Q. Isn't Feng shui just an alternate design philosophy ?

A. Certainly not. The furniture placement and accessorizing aspect is just one part of Feng shui. The core of this subject is about grasping energies hidden within our physical environment. The art of cleansing and consecrating spaces is another vital part of Feng shui. Directionality is, of course, the most commonly understood facet. Besides this, *Dowsing, Space Clearing, Astrology, Oriental Diagnosis* etc. are some of the other valid extensions of Feng shui. All these aspects together makeup true Feng shui philosophy, which is --- *living your current lifetime to the fullest.*

Q. What would be so unique about a Feng shui decorator's advice versus that of a good interior designer ?

A. For one, your designer's focus would be on the outward appearance and embellishment of the space in question. The basis most probably would be pictures of interiors that you like, the "style" you want expressed etc. Color, lighting, textures, all an integral part of any good interior design effort.

What a Feng shui practitioner does, is however, a little different. He/ she addresses the *"Soul of the Space"*, with respect to your unique cosmological makeup. His/her design and decoration advice is highly personalized and solely targeting for greatest harmony, and its consequent benefits to you.

> **A designer with a Feng shui perspective will see to both Aesthetics and Accord**

THE FIVE- ELEMENT THEORY

The chart shows how these elements
can be interpreted in usable terms.
Harnessing the spirit, qualities and characteristics
of these energies in architecture/ interior design
is what this theory is all about.

WOOD	wooden furniture, Bamboo screens	green	vertical lines, rectangular shapes,
METAL	metal furniture, wrought iron decorative pieces	white, gold,	circular shapes, cylindrical forms
EARTH	terracotta urns	yellow, ochre	square shapes, cubes,
WATER	fountains, aquariums	black, deep blue	wavy lines, irregular patterns
FIRE	bright flowers	red	triangular, star shapes,

Q. Symbolism seems to be quite an indispensable part of Feng shui. Is this true ?

A. Chinese people, till date laid a lot of emphasis on symbols and metaphors. For them each word, syllable, object, has a literal and a symbolic meaning. Even their numbers have deeper meanings, like the sound of the number *"four"* is similar to the word for *"Death"*, so it is a rather unpopular number. Ancient Chinese coins tied together with a ribbon are symbolic of wealth, some birds, plants and fruits too figure in the "good luck" charm category. Even pot plants, candle stands, pottery and fans can help *Ch'i* circulate effectively when strategically placed. Experts in Feng shui are frequently asked how such basically mundane objects, pose as barriers against bad *"Shar Ch'i"*. Each item is carefully selected for the particular kind of energy it represents (wind/ water/ fire/ metal/ earth) and its symbolic meaning. The right object can yield some very powerful and surprising results.

Q. Are dragons a valid part of Feng shui ?

A. The Chinese have always considered the dragon- *"Lung"*, a most auspicious creature. It is a metaphor for the energy of the landscape. Particular formations denote the *"Path of the dragons and Tigers"*, *"flow of the dragon"*. To defy the dragon would result in "bleeding the dragon", meaning inviting disaster. In lay terms, this would mean building with disregard for the local conditions, trees etc... basically committing an ecological offense while building.(Plate no.7)

Q. How bad can wrongly done Feng shui be ?

A. Bad Feng shui brings illness and disaster, accidents and financial loss. It can cause opportunities to slip away, careers to fade, wealth to be squandered, and reputations to collapse. Harmful energy coming into your house, beams over beds, toilets in the wrong places etc. are all manifestations of bad Feng shui. Wrongly placed enhancers like water features, chimes etc. also can inflict damage by way of health problems. Commonly felt "bad Feng shui" is when things just keep going wrong, and you feel at a loss to cope with stresses.(Plate no. 10)

A good consultant would be able to tell you whether your problems can be solved with only Feng shui, or if there is need to perform *"Smudging"* or *"Space Clearing"* and/ or *"Dowsing"*, (all independent, adjunct sciences), in addition to eradicate the ROOT of your difficulties.

Do not get taken up with
Spurious, and Erroneous "improving" techniques,
in the name of
"Cosmic Energy Science" / "Modern Vaastu"-etc.

Authentic "Compass School" Feng shui will involve:

- Use of a "*Luo Pan*" (Elaborate Chinese reference compass).
- The birth dates of the user/s as well as the building.
- Charting the "*Gua*" of the space w.r.t users.
- Detailed "*Wu Xing*" analysis & recommendations for each part of space.
- Drawing up of the "*Lo-Shu*" magic square for determining planetary effects on the built space.

Authentic "Form School" Feng Shui would involve:

- Site study and solutions from the "Form school" ideal configuration, point of view (Plate no. 6)
- Charting of the *Chi* flow wither and without the space in question
- Recommendations based Green Dragon & White Tiger and Red Phoenix and Black Turtle concepts.
- Locational plus and minus points w.r.t. to the four celestial animals

Authentic "Black Sect" Feng shui would involve:
- Determing the Real Front Entrance or gateway
- The "*Ba-gua*" energy blue print of each space
- Ascertaining the Nine sectors of any space along with the aspiration they signify
- Pointing out which *'Gua/s'* are missing due to any irregularity if any
- Suggesting mundane/transcendental cures
- Intuitive *Feeling Out* of space

BASIC PRINCIPLES & REMEDIES

Q. Can I have the basic principles of Feng shui, in brief ?

A. *"TAO"* (Dow) is the essential conceptual principle of Feng shui. It is a process and principal linking man with the universe. Other fundamental concepts are, the balance of the *"Yin"* and *"Yang"* elements and the harmony of the *"Five Elements"* (Plate nos.1,2 & 3).

All things feminine, negative and passive, cool colours, darkness, night, moon, shadow, soft materials and a static disposition represent the *YIN* quality. Masculine, positive and active qualities, warm colours, brightness, day, sun, and light, hard materials and an active disposition represent *YANG*. The Chinese believe that by combining the five elements - Fire, Water, Earth, Metal, Wood in different quantities, it is possible to create all the permutations of nature. Their inherent properties and interrelationships are analyzed, in Feng shui, with respect to a space and the elemental makeup of its users. (Plate no 3, 4 & 5)

GENERIC SHAPES & FORMS
OF THE FIVE ELEMENTS

Metal

Water

Fire

Wood

Earth

These principles permeate all of Feng shui practice, irrespective of which school is being followed. They are fundamental to understanding the Chinese view of the universe and the forces that affect human destiny.

Q. How are *YIN* and *YANG* used in practical terms ?

A. Feng shui basically tries to ascertain the nature and degree of energy in balances in the space in question and then applies the particular element necessary in its symbolic form to harmonize the situation.

YIN and *YANG* (Plate nos.1 & 2) provide the backbone to an initial overview of space from a Feng shui point of view.

Yang living environments would include living in small flats, crowded localities, working in a brightly lit environment. A *yang* interior is typically very well lit, has bright colors in the upholstery or paintings, uses shiny materials like steel, aluminum glazed ceramic tiles. The diffused nature of Yin energy on the other hand can be represented by a rural or semi urban location, large spacious homes, dimly lit spaces, use of plenty of wood or modern plastics.

Q. Feng shui is commonly understood as just placing mirrors & chimes all over the place. How far is this true ?

A. As with the most deep of philosophies, misinterpretation and misinformation is quite the rule. It takes a lot of the correct kind of exposure for people to grasp and appreciate the myriad meanings of Feng shui.

Mirrors and chimes do feature a lot in several Feng shui suggestions, but they are just and miniscule part of the overhaul involved in Feng shui application. **Specific mundane and esoteric "*Cures*" are used to symbolically unblock energy meridians though their positioning.**

Q. How accurate are the popular "*ANIMAL SIGN*" predictions ?

A. They are as accurate as Sun- Sign predictions, giving general guidelines for human characteristics in relation to their destiny. They are commonly used to assess compatibilities between people, in a qualitative manner.

Q. What does my "Animal Sign" reflect ?

A. This sign reflects the typical characteristics of the Chinese astrological "animal" indicated in your personality. These are further modified by the element relating to the year of your birth. For example, a person born in 1965 would be a *wood snake*; therefore 1999 would be good year for him, because 1999 is the year of a wood rabbit. You must, however, remember to take the "*animal*" indicated purely as a *metaphor.* (Appendix- B)

Q. Can my "Animal Sign", according to Chinese astrology affect Feng shui solutions for me ?

A. Besides there being a right place for everything, the Chinese believe there is also a **right time. Astrology thus is an inescapable adjunct to all Feng shui**

practices. Unlike western astrology, which is month oriented, a person's **year of birth** is the determining factor in Chinese astrology.

(Appendix- B). Knowing which of the 12 animal signs you are is essential, according to the Chinese, for choosing worthy partners, spouses, and good times. For example, a home missing in the marriage portion may also be bad for people born in the years of the Ox and the Tiger.

Q. What does my "*BIRTH ELEMENT*" reflect ?

A. Each person is born under the influence of one of the five elements of Chinese philosophy - wood, metal, fire, water, and earth.

This can be found in the Chinese Almanac - or the *Thousand-year calendar* (The "*Tong Shu*"). In Feng shui terms, this element is of key significance.
(Appendix-B)

Q. Exactly how can this help in my home or office interiors ?

A. The Five elements represent specific energies, which relate closely to their natural characteristics.

Their **compatibility cycle** is based on a free flowing circular moment linking the elements in a productive sequence. Their **incompatibility** cycle is similarly sequenced. (Plate no. 3)

You should choose the colors / materials / textures of your birth year element and / or of the element that produces your element (according to the

IDEAL FENG SHUI CONFIGURATION FOR A BUILDING LOOKING OUTWARDS

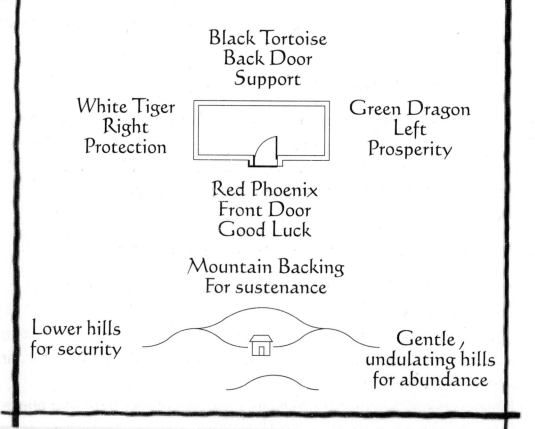

Black Tortoise
Back Door
Support

White Tiger
Right
Protection

Green Dragon
Left
Prosperity

Red Phoenix
Front Door
Good Luck

Mountain Backing
For sustenance

Lower hills
for security

Gentle,
undulating hills
for abundance

Plate No. 6

"*Productive Cycle*"). This will ensure that you will be able to tap into the qualities of the elements that will be most helpful for you personally. The positive energy benefits can be availed even by your choice of clothing and accessories. (Plate nos.4 & 5)

Q. Mirrors are seen to be a large part of Feng shui. What do they do ?

A. *Ch'i* energy behaves like light waves; therefore mirrors can be used to deflect the waves, (just as light bounces off a mirror). They guide and direct *Ch'i*, enabling it to flow in the desired direction. There are several varied uses of mirrors in Feng shui. E.g., a long corridor can be made Feng shui friendly just by putting mirrors on either side of it, thereby slowing down the *Ch'i* flow. Large mirrors however absorb the *Ch'i*, as they create the illusion that the space extends beyond the wall.

Q. Can any mirror be used for these purposes ?

A. The size of a mirror should be such that it is large enough for the function. The important thing to remember is that, they should not be at a height that your reflection appears with the head cut off.

Any mirror used for Feng shui purposes should also, preferably have auspicious dimensions according to the *Feng shui Ruler* (a measuring device with degrees of auspicious and inauspicious marked out in linear dimensions).

Do not use mirror tiles instead as they break up the image and thus cause harm to the person or relationship reflected. The mirror frame should also be looked at from the "Five Element" color/ material point of view.

(Plate no.4)

> ### Specific mundane and esoteric "Cures" are used to symbolically unblock energy meridians though their positioning

Q. Why are wind chimes so popular in Feng shui ?

A. The ringing sound of a wind chime or bell has the effect of vibrating the air, which in turn stimulates the *Chi* in the area. This has a cleansing effect on the space. It is important to choose a **metallic** wind chime that resonates well, with a pleasing sound.

Q. Can any sound in the building be beneficial ?

A. No. Only sounds that are pleasing to the ear and melodious in effect are good. They help to enhance the potentially beneficial vibrations of a space. So, you may want to evaluate the sound of your doorbell in this light; or alter the telephone ringer to be less harsh.

Q. Which is the best place for me to hang a wind chime ?

A. Like I mentioned above, the placement of a wind chime needs to be looked at on the basis of a broad *Pa- kua* categorization of the space, or set of spaces (Plate no. 8). A wind chime represents the element of metal, in addition to being a powerful *Ch'i* activator. Only a correctly located wind-chime can produce the desired results. (Plate no. 12)

Q. Is there any place I should definitely *not* hang a wind chime, in the house ?

A. Yes; never hang metal chimes in the East and Southeast parts of your room or house.

This is a compass school inference, as the East and Southeast symbolize the element of Wood and according to the Destructive Cycle of elements (plate no. 3) Metal cuts or Destroys wood. Therefore all metallic objects are unsuitable for placing in these sectors.

Q. What are the main taboos in Feng shui ?

A. The single most important thing to watch for are harmful energy lines ("*Shar-Ch'i*) coming from **sharp edges**, a single tree, pole etc., pointing at your front door (Plate no.10). These are called "*poison arrows*". These could lead to sickness, misfortune and disharmony in relationships.

BASIC "FORM SCHOOL", FENG SHUI SITE LOCATION

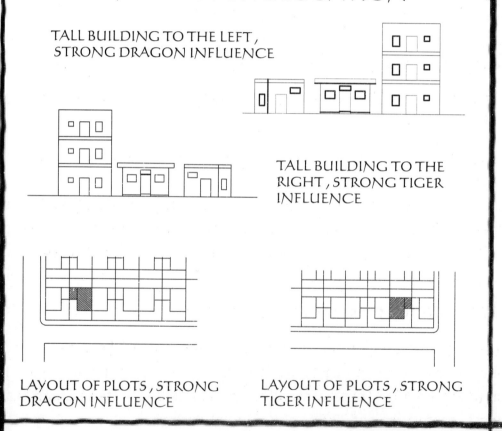

TALL BUILDING TO THE LEFT, STRONG DRAGON INFLUENCE

TALL BUILDING TO THE RIGHT, STRONG TIGER INFLUENCE

LAYOUT OF PLOTS, STRONG DRAGON INFLUENCE

LAYOUT OF PLOTS, STRONG TIGER INFLUENCE

Plate No. 7

Apart from this, sitting, sleeping, working under exposed overhead beams is considered very bad for health. Having your main door opening on to a congested space, and having toilets in the southwest sector of your home are also all common taboos in Feng shui.

Q. Can I protect my house from these *"Poison Arrows"*?

A. Yes. By hanging a "*PA-KUA*" mirror (Plate no.12) above your front door, or by changing the orientation of the door itself.

> The most important thing to watch for
> are harmful energy lines ("*Shar-Ch'i*)
> coming from sharp edges--
> a single tree, pole etc., pointing at your front door

Q. Can light fixtures be good enough to energize any sector ?

A. Artificial light is best used in combination with natural light in order to establish the emotional tone of a room. It is also an easy way of introducing color into an interior scheme. This can be the color of the fitting itself or the bulb color.

Q. What are the good fortune symbols of Feng shui, and how effective are they?

A. Traditional Chinese good fortune symbols come in various forms-auspicious calligraphies, figurines made of wood, brass, *Shou Shan* stone, glass/ crystal, image overlays on transparent plastic etc. They all are potent and powerful when correctly placed.

Some of the more common uses for Feng shui symbols are:

- Help love life, marriage success, and solicit blessings of elders.
- Improve career mobility, business luck.
- Infuse positive energy into your children's mental, intellectual & emotional health.
- Contribute to good health and longevity of whole family
- Foster harmony and peace in family.
- Open out opportunities for prosperity.

Q. What is "*Space Clearing*" ?

A. It is the **art of purifying spaces and making them Sacred.** Clutter is what is removed in any space clearing. Clutter is not only the commonly understood "*mess*", but also "*Stuck- Energy*", undesirable psychic debris... basically static low-level energy that accumulates everywhere, but especially in corners, nooks and edges.

Moving, flowing energy is healthy and very often, when you feel trapped in some issue in your life, there is always a corresponding "*stuckness*" in some part of your home. *Space Clearing* is used very effectively to clear out the heavier, undesirable vibrations that are often attached to unhappy memories.

Q. Is Space Clearing a part of Feng shui ?

A. Energetically, all events and activities inside buildings get recorded in its walls, floor, ceiling, furniture etc. A common example of this is when you enter a room where there has just been an argument. The tension is palpable in the air. The all the surrounding inanimate things absorb the residue of these energy ripples.

How much "*Stuck Energy*" builds up in a space depends on the "*Feng shui-Index*" of the place (a rating giving the Feng shui compliance).

So, by creating good Feng shui, you can affect a substantial part of the energetics, thus consciously creating a clean, healthy and happy atmosphere for your family. Space clearing enhances the higher levels of vibrations in the air; making any Feng shui changes or enhancements work more smoothly and deeply. **It is however a fully valid, independent subject--- that is an extremely useful adjunct to Feng shui.**

"Space clearing" enhances the
higher levels of vibrations in the air;
making any Feng shui changes or enhancements
work more smoothly and deeply

COMMON METHODS & TOOLS

Q. Are there many versions of Feng shui ?

A. Feng shui has evolved over several centuries and several schools of thought emerged within the framework of the same fundamental principles. The prominent ones are:

FORM SCHOOL: This school concentrates mainly on the configuration of the landscape, watercourses, and contours. The relationship between the individual dwelling with the surrounding physical formations is what is seen in this version. Four *celestial animals* symbolize the four directions of the compass. (Plate no. 6). This school of Feng shui lays down evaluations of "*Dragon-Tiger*" configurations, and looks deeply into identifying and negating poison arrows in alignments. (Plate no.7).

COMPASS SCHOOL: This school uses the eight Trigrams of the I *Ching*, the *Pa-Kua* diagram(Plate no. 8), and the *Lo-Shu* magic square for its evaluations.

The approach here is to assess the Feng shui- Index of spaces/locations, the *Ch'i* flow and the planetary influences on buildings. This version involves detailed computations with an elaborate compass called the *Luo - Pan*.(Plate no.9).

BLACK HAT SECT FENG SHUI: This is a relatively recent school of thought, predominantly practiced in the United States. It was developed by Dr. Thomas Lin Yun, and is a hybrid of Tibetan Buddhism, Taoism and intuitive Feng shui. There is a distinct spiritual leaning in this version of Feng shui.

Q. Which of these methods effective for modern day use ?

A. All the methodologies are based on common fundamental concepts. The difference lies in the approach and not the aim. The effectiveness of each depends largely on the capabilities of the practitioner. Quite often, an *optimum* combination of methods is what is most effective.

Q. Which of these is the easiest to learn for a beginner ?

A. The *Black Hat Sect* School Of Feng shui is the simplest one to apply, for a learner. This school of Feng shui believes that every manmade space has its own unique "Energy Blue print" - called the "*Ba- Gua*" of the space. This is in the form of a bubble diagram with nine sectors representing nine life stations or aspirations of Human Life. It does not require the use of a compass for

"*Pa - Kua*" Model
The indispensable energetic overlay of Feng shui

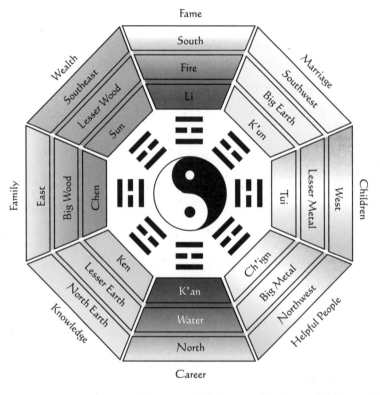

Plate No. 8

directions, and is based on orienting the *Ba-Gua* with respect to the entrance of a space.

Q. What are the tools used in Feng shui ?

A. The primary tools are:

- The *Luo Pan*- or Chinese reference compass. It is an extraordinary device that contains a cache of Feng shui secret formulae. These clues and symbols indicate good and bad Feng shui, but need great expertise to fathom and interpret. (Plate no.9)
- The *Pa- Kua* diagram-an energetic spatial overlay. This is an elaborate eight-sided symbol, which has *I-Ching Trigrams* on each side in addition to a host of other information about the characteristics of each direction of the compass. (Plate no. 8)

Q. What are the essential pieces of information one needs for an accurate Feng shui analysis ?

A. An accurate assessment would require:

- The **date/s of birth** of the principal occupants of the space to be considered.
- A location map of the whole are in addition to **detailed floor plans** would also be required.

- In case of a corporate project, a broad company profile and objectives along with the birth data of the manger/s is needed.
- In case of a Residential project, the family structure occupying the premises is also needed additionally.
- For a Feng shui evaluation of a Franchise Shop or Showroom, the products/ services for sale and the real owner/s birth date is needed.

In all cases, the age of the building and the date of occupation are essential for accuracy of solutions. Other buildings, such as Schools, Banks, Factories would also require all of the abovementioned basic data.

Q. Is Feng shui useful for urban situations, which have hardly any natural environment ?

A. In the urban landscape, roads are to be considered the channels of *Ch'i* and buildings representative of landforms. The *Four Celestial Animals* symbolize the directions of the compass.(Plate no. 6) These principles are used to "*read into*" any urban scenario and interpret in terms of these animals. **This kind of an analysis is very prophetic in telling whether a particular building located the way it is, would augur well**. Real estate agents are the biggest clients, as they are always prospecting for auspicious sites, offices, plotted houses and apartments.

In the urban landscape, roads are to be considered the channels of *Ch'i* and buildings representative of landforms

A "*Luo Pan*"
The essential Feng shui reference compass

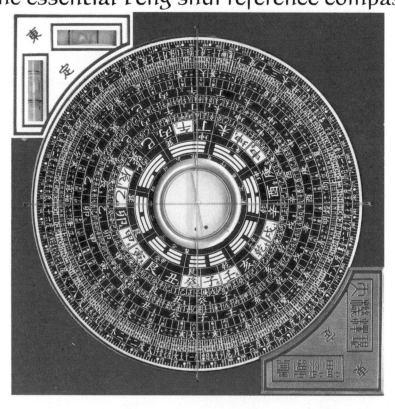

Plate No. 9

SPECIFIC UTILITIES & ADVANTAGES

Q. What are the popular benefits of Feng shui application ?

A. Feng shui is gaining increasing popularity the world over. A large number of non- Asians are looking up to Feng shui to help **De-stress their lives and make their homes auspicious havens for them.** Essentially oriental in its makeup, Feng shui is easily acceptable to the Asian, who is able to grasp all the symbolism effortlessly. The core purpose of Feng shui is of course to make our lives richer, happier and full of abundance.

Specific applications of this ancient art are—

(i) To stimulate your wealth stars, inviting potential prosperity "*stars*". enhancing your money luck .

(ii) To live a healthier and more energetic life by nullifying /lifting the stress producing elements in your surroundings (Plate no. 10).

(iii) To nourish your children's health and education.

(iv)　To have a peaceful, harmonious family life at home.

(v)　Get some help in the interior décor of your home with the aesthetic principles of *Yin* and *Yang* to achieve a balanced and invigorating home atmosphere.(Plate nos. 1 & 2).

vi)　To unblock the flow of fortune into your business premises and to protect your investments

vii)　To get ahead in your career; by getting the right job break, or getting recognition.

viii)　To open up hidden opportunities, remove obstacles in the oath of your progress.

ix)　To strengthen your marriage, smoothen and enrich relationships.

Q. Can Feng shui be used to help a floundering marriage ?

A. Usually a situation like this would never arise if the Feng shui of the house had been correctly positioned in the first place- including the sleeping direction of the husband and wife. In such cases, suitable Feng shui enhancements made to the "*Marriage Sector*" invariably yields success.

Q. Are there any "Quick - Fix" tips for better health, with Feng shui ?

A. For better health for yourself and your family, concentrate on the eastern section of your house and of all rooms. Even the garden can be taken into purview. The eastern sector is associated with the element Wood- so putting a healthy green plant, or introducing green in upholstery or accessories activates this region. Good Feng shui in the east will thus represent the overall well being of the family. Traditional Chinese symbols of longevity can also be incorporated in the décor. Clearing Clutter in your surroundings is probably the most inexpensive and effective way to de- stress yourself, and feel healthier.

Q. Can Feng shui aid in matters of the heart- viz. Love ?

A. Feng shui can bring good vibrations to romance and marriage, smoothing over and enhancing relationships and thereby bringing happiness to your personal life. Few common ways are:

- Introducing red, white and pink in the South West sectors of the house and bedroom.
- Auspicious calligraphy indicating happiness,
- A pair of mandarin Ducks with a red string tied around both of them.

Q. How can Feng shui make me more successful / popular ?

A. By installing a bright light in your southern sector you will enhance your personal fame and reputation - the brighter the light the better. Green or Red colored decorations and candle stands with red candles help immensely too. You can perhaps frame your degrees and certificates and hang them in this location of your home or office. Prints of the auspicious *Red Phoenix* boost personal fame tremendously.

Q. Can Feng shui help with my children's success and happiness ?

A. Feng shui can come in handy in alleviating some difficulties with children. This may involve changing the children's sleeping or sitting position. Activating the west sector of the House as a whole and the child's room in particular with metal wind chimes, white colored decorations would help. (Plate no.12)

Q. What are the key advantages of Feng shui in business ?

A. In business, observing Feng shui rules in the selection and design of your premises is a way to:

- Create growth opportunities, synergetic impulse.
- Elevate the business profile and your standing in the community.
- Attract customers, raise profits, and expand turnover.
- Protect your investments by setting right any damaging aspects of you business premises.
- Introduce an atmosphere, where employees stay loyal and a pervasive aura of goodwill creates smooth working relationships.

In places where the population is predominantly Chinese—such as Hong Kong, Taiwan, and Singapore-businessmen who want that extra edge unfailingly

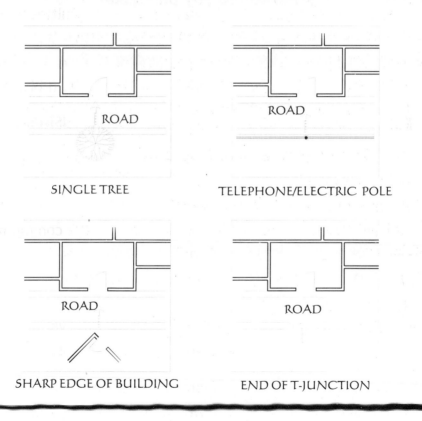

"POISON ARROWS"
in the urban landscape

SINGLE TREE

TELEPHONE/ELECTRIC POLE

SHARP EDGE OF BUILDING

END OF T-JUNCTION

Plate No. 10

consult Feng shui masters in getting their yearly alignment in the most auspicious manner. Feng shui is used extensively in all kinds of corporate settings with an unfailing success rate globally.

Q. Can color be targeted to aid any particular problem/s ?

A. The therapeutic effect of color is a commonly grasped thing. What is not known is, how the creative use of color according to Feng shui can actually alleviate a serious sickness and mitigate a grave family emergency. For example if a young child constantly keeps unwell, the introduction of metallic white and gilded objects on the western wall of the western most room can solve the problem to a great extent. Even a picture of the child in a suitable metallic frame can work!

Such beneficial color guidelines can be worked out easily by consulting the "*Pa-Kua*" diagram (plate no 8). These are very potent guidelines and are the most popular Feng shui techniques for alleviating any problem.

APPLICATION FOR AUSPICIOUS HOUSE/APARTMENT DESIGN

Q. What does it mean, to have my house *"Feng shui-ed"*?

A. The assessment of the positive and negative feature of your house is the primary Feng shui purpose. This involves charting the movement of energies from the surrounding landscape and through your house. **Suggestions for optimum placement of furniture, decor and colour schemes** are also an integral part of Feng shui advice for a house.

There is **very rarely need to break** any wall or alter the position of doors/windows. Feng shui has ways for you to get its benefits with simple practical spatial adjustments that are quite inexpensive too. Since it offers a mix of activation and protection, the amount of Feng shui you may want to dabble with is quite flexible. You can also conveniently phase out the additions/alterations over a logical period of time.

ORIENTING YOUR HOME

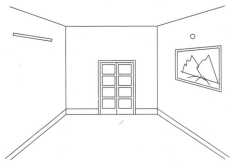

ENTRANCE AREA
Hold compass
Standing at door
looking out

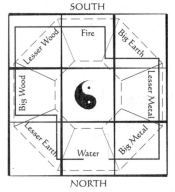

SOUTH

Lesser Wood · Fire · Big Earth

Big Wood · Lesser Metal

Lesser Earth · Water · Big Metal

NORTH

Divide your floor plan into 9
squares and schematically
overlay
the Pa-kua diagram

Such a Luo-Pan compass
is generally used

> Feng shui has ways for you
> to get its benefits with
> simple, practical spatial adjustments
> that are quite inexpensive too

Q. What is the first step for using Feng shui in my house ?

A. The first step in Feng shui house design is to segment the house into *nine sectors* corresponding to the *eight compass directions*, leaving one in the center.(Plate no.8)

Each of the sectors corresponds to one of the compass directions - either the primary directions (north, south, ease, and west) or one of the secondary directions (Northeast, southeast, northwest, and southwest). You can use an approximate sketch plan of your house for this for approximate locations. (Plate no.11)

Q. Can I incorporate Feng shui in specific rooms alone ?

A. Yes. It is possible to consider any room absolutely independently for Feng shui purposes. The principle divisions or "*sectors*" should be made in the same manner. (Plate no.11)

Q. Can Feng shui be easily applied to an existing design ?

A. As I have stated earlier, the best part about the art of Feng shui is that it is so friendly and flexible. **Your choices and decisions are paramount.**

This philosophy can be seen in the fact that Feng shui concentrates on the "*Comfort Level*" of the Space. **Now, this comfort is both yours forward to your house and your house backwards to you.**

What this means is that it is equally important that the vital energies flowing through your home be kept activated and "happy", as much as you "*feeling*", good about the way you have done-up your home interior. It is therefore, quite easy to apply Feng shui to any existing situation effortlessly and economically too!

> It is equally important that
> the vital energies flowing
> through your home
> be kept activated and "happy",

> As much as you "feeling", good
> about the way you have
> done- up your home interior.

Q. How long will the effects last ?

A. As long as what you have done, does not contraindicate the auspicious and/ or inauspicious-yearly planetary influence on your house. This can only be determined by complex computations. In any case making your home, aesthetically pleasing, energetically balanced and free of negative elements is going to be **permanently beneficial.**

Putting in any efforts towards creating accord in the energies embedded in your home would definitely be richly rewarding. A kind of a *"snowballing motion"* gets set-up wherein your family and you harmonize and an overall *"Good Feeling"* prevails.

What can, however heighten the experience is, if you maintain your "inner Feng shui" as well—that is physical, emotional & spiritual well- being.

Q. The home is quite often a gallery to exhibit one's self Worth. How does Feng shui deal with this aspect ?

A. A home is a mirror of our inner self. This is quite evident in the way contemporary homes are decorated. It is human nature to have pride in his possessions. Residential interior decoration projects also often display unabashed "*Designer*" icons of affluence, as extensions of how those people dress.

Feng shui takes a very constructive view of this, but insists that whatever you do should be in keeping the universal principles of *Yin/ Yang* balance and the harmony of the five colours. (Plate nos.1 & 2) However, there are several people who are oblivious of their houses, considering them mere backdrops against which they live their lives. That is, of course the fartherest from truth.

Each room of your house requires our attention, with respect to some careful thought paid to their layouts and décor. And each and every effort, however humble, should be "*Feng shui-ed*" at some time or the other.

Q. Can I have a permanent Feng shui solution for the design of my house, one that remains favorable for a long time ?

A. The practice has 2 dimensions- a **Space Dimension**, which concerns the **Physical Environment**, and a **Time dimension**, which concerns changing atmospheric forces. The intangible forces, man-made and natural in our environment are constantly changing. Thus Feng shui as an art of attaining balance is not static too. It requires regular adaptation. The urban scenario especially is always changing with more constructions, alterations to the landscape etc. Age of buildings too is an important consideration in Feng shui, so also is the time of making a Move.

A true Feng shui practitioner will be always alert to the need for change however small it may need to be in order to accommodate the various shifting earth and cosmic vibrations. Successful companies like "Swire McClaine" employ the services of a Feng shui consultant on a regular basis, and make suitable yearly alterations to their corporate properties.

Q. I want to buy a plot that is most auspicious for my family. How can Feng shui help ?

A. For a site to be auspicious, it must have access to, or be near, a good, strong supply and flow of *Ch'i*. (Plate no.6)

Do not, for example, buy property that is hemmed in by tall buildings, or land that faces or is close to huge man - made structures such as electricity pylons, transmission towers, power stations, or water tanks. Also avoid land facing straight roads (especially at the end of a Cul - de - sac), railroad tracks, and T-junctions. These bring Cutting *Ch'i*, which is difficult to correct, as do buildings with crosses or steeples. In Feng shui, anything straight that is pointed at the land or home should be avoided. (Plate no.10)

Be wary of such structures and buildings, and scrupulously avoid buying a piece of land that is near or adjacent to them, or worse, facing directly onto them.

Q. Which is the ideal place to have a water feature ?

A. This depends on for what Feng shui purpose, if at all, you want to add a water feature. The north sector of any room is good. If you are considering the entrance foyer, then take care that it is at the left of the main door, while *looking out*.

Q. How does one Feng shui the Kitchen ?

A. Traditionally the kitchen is the social center of the house and the focus of many domestic activities. In Feng shui the kitchen is associated with the nourishment and health of the family. The Chinese believe that a correctly

POWERFUL SYMBOLS
OF FENG SHUI

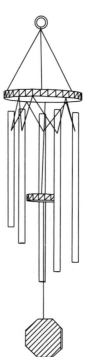

A "PA-KUA" MIRROR

A WIND CHIME

Plate No. 12

positioned cooking stove of the home can help overcome several other defects in the layout.

Since a modern kitchen is full of appliances, mostly related to the five elements, the direction they face is quite important. The cooker especially should not face either the front or back door or be fartherest from the dishwasher or sink. Clutter should be avoided, Keep all edges rounded.

Q. Are cupboards with fully mirrored shutters okay to use ?

A. This depends on the location of such cupboards with respect to the specific room they are in. The mirrored shutters can be uses advantageously, in locations where full-length mirrors are suggested. They can also be quite harmful in case they reflect any undesirable element like a toilet or an edge of a wall. Its best however not to use such cupboards inside the bedroom itself as the presence of any mirrors here is considered bad according to Feng shui. They can be safely used in a separate dressing room.

Q. Which is the best place to locate the television in a house ?

A. In the western sector of your room, as that is the *Metal* sector. Placing your T.V here will activate both your creativity and energize your children, making it a positive force in your home.

Q. Is there any particular good direction my house should face according to Feng shui ?

A. As you may know some houses are more favorable for certain people, but quite detrimental to others this is the function of the house facing a particular direction. There is a number called the "*Kua*" number which when calculated will guide you in determining your based directions. There are also charts available to tell you whether you are an *East group* or a *West group* person. This information when collated yields your *Best Direction* - i.e., **the most auspicious compass orientation for you.** If your house faces this specific direction, then you will have good health, wealth and harmony in life. You can refer to the chart given in the Appendix-B, to find your particular direction.

If perchance your house faces a Bad Direction then it is advisable to simply try to enhance all aspects of your Best Direction WITHIN the house, so as to overcome to a large extent any negative effects of front door orientation. Remember, in Feng shui, it is the overall sum of good points Vs. bad points that is relevant for best benefits to the occuparnts.

Q. How critical is the orientation of the bed in a bedroom ?

A. The bed is the haven of refuge and relaxation for all of us. It is where we recuperate our energies and completely unwind our bodies. It is, but natural that Feng shui considers the positioning of our sleeping place one of the most vital things to adhere to. Ideally, a bed should be diagonally opposite the door with the feet on the door side.

The next best location is on the sidewall. In case of a master bed the bed head is to be oriented towards the *best direction* of the main breadwinner of the family. (Appendix-B)

Q. Is there any harm in having a work area in the bedroom ?

A. This is a very common thing nowadays, with the burgeoning numbers of people who operate work from their homes. It is not particularly desirable, according to Feng shui. A solution is to screen off your table and computer from the sight of the bed. The operating logic here is that, a workspace with its associated gadgetry is very *Yang;* a bedroom however, is supposed to be the most *Yin* place in the house—so the two don't mix well.

> A kind of a snowballing motion gets set- up wherein your family and you harmonize, and an overall "Good Feeling" prevails.

Q. What are the implications of irregularity in plan shape ?

A. All the extensions of your plan, if under the same roof count as one space. Most houses, apartments, or offices are irregular in shape. The implications of the irregularity vary, depending on the amount and kind of variation.

Broadly speaking, there are two types of asymmetrical shapes -

a) Those with parts missing - (indentation that is less than half the length of the building

b) Those with extensions (part/s which sticks out). You need to draw up the biggest rectangle over your plan and then see which portions fall into the above two categories.

Either way, it means that there would be some imbalance in the specific areas of your life the missing part/s represent according to the *Pa-Kua*. Extensions are considered good, as long as they don't overpower the main plan.(Plate 8 & 11)

Q. How much importance should one give to the orientation of the front door of a house ?

A. A lot of your family's fortunes depend on whether the main door is auspicious for you. In almost every traditional culture, the entrance to any space is a celebrated affair.

In addition it is considered rather sacred too, as it is believed that good energies and Heavenly blessings come in primarily from the main door. Conversely, a wrongly facing door could spell disaster to the occupants. This concept stretches to offices, shops, factories etc. too. Apart from the orientation, the shape, size, color, design of the entrance door are all significant factors, according to Feng shui.

The Orientation of the
Main door of a house has unparalleled importance.

Feng shui practitioners can
read into the fortunes of a household
by simply taking a " Luo- Pan " reading of its front door.

Q. What are the best locations for toilets in a house ?

A. Toilets are the bane of Feng shui and are seen as necessary evils. Symbolically, a toilet represents the water element. This means that it should definitely not be in the Fire zones -the southern areas. Best locations are **East and Southeast**.

Q. Which directions should one keep gilded objects for best effect ?

A. The West, and the North- west areas of your room, house, office or shop. Even gilded picture frames and brass light fixture can come in this category.

Q. Which is the best place to keep crystal objects?

A. In the Southwest, or Northeast of any room, preferably well lit for best advantage of their *"Earth Ch'i"* energies.

Q. A farmhouse is generally laid out in an open piece of land, with flexibility of external development: So can one be designed with ideal Feng shui ?

A. It is possible to have a majority of Feng shui factors designed favorably, if a project is in collaboration with a Feng shui consultant right from the start. A farmhouse does indeed present such an opportunity. However, how much the user/s gain from the theoretically correct placement would depend on:

- Solutions based on their particular "*birth*" and "*animal*" signs.
- The extent advanced Feng shui formulae have been applied.
- "Trinity" of luck--Heaven Luck (Time), and Man Luck (Action), of the user.

Q. When faulty house layouts are stacked one above the other, as in a high rise apartment complex, do the "faults" also multiply ?

A. This will depend to a large extent on what exactly the faults are. But, in most cases, the bad effects would be restricted to the individual flat only.

The apartment complex would be affected as a whole, by its position with respect to the surrounding landscape, and the placement of the common utilities such as Swimming pool, Generator Room, and Community Building etc.

Q. Does the Feng shui for an Apartment/ Flat differ from that for a plotted house ?

A. No. The principles and techniques would all be the same, irrespective of which size of house is being considered. Even single rooms living accommodations, like hostel rooms, dormitories, etc can be greatly benefited by a little Feng shui.

Q. Are there any special rules for residential offices ?

A. The generic concepts would all apply. The only difference in such a situation can be incorporating all the associated office equipment and/ or infrastructure. What is important to note here is that an office is essentially a very *"Yang"* place, but the home is a mixture of *Yang and Yin* activities. This basic dichotomy has to be handled with care, so as to keep the harmony and balance. Even the way colors, materials and textures are applied could vary for a pure residential accommodation and an Office cum Home.
(Plate nos. 1 & 2)

RESOURCES

Most of you might need further clarification on several aspects of Feng shui that relate to your specific situation, but do not want to take on any elaborate and expensive consultation. Economy and circumstantial constraints too deter many from going much further with a full- fledged Feng shui appraisal of their premises.

"FENG SHUI- ADVANTAGE FOR YOU"™ is a professionally managed, confidential, and Value-For-Money, Help line, consultancy service that gives you **practical, insightful, and convenient solutions** to all your Feng shui needs, keeping the abovementioned factors in mind.

You may contact the following address for details. Answers are in the form of fax/ email / registered post. Samples of questions received in this Help line are given in Appendix-1.

ESOTERIC ARCHITECTURE
E- 904, Chittaranjan Park, New Delhi -110019
Tel: 91-11-646 7176, 622 7176, Fax: 91-11-641 7176,
E- mail: nma@vsnl.com
"Power Decoration"™, is a, soon to be commenced
Mail Order service that will provide a wide- ranging choice of
Feng shui tools, and exclusive accessories.

LIST OF PLATES

APPENDIX-A

A SAMPLE OF QUESTIONS RECEIVED IN THE ABOVE MENTIONED "FENG SHUI- ADVANTAGE TO YOU"™ HELPLINE

Q. My wife and I have contradictory "Good Directions". Whose should be considered for Feng shui purpose ?

Q. I live in a flat with very little natural light and ventilation. Can Feng shui help make my house more auspicious ?

Q. The main door of my house opens directly onto the staircase area. Can this affect me adversely, and what can I do about it ?

Q. I heard that the front door should not be in line with the rear door. In our house the entrance lobby has French doors on the opposite side, opening onto the lawn. Is this Okay ?

Q. I live in an old house full of exposed timber beams and girders. How do I nullify their bad effects ?

Q. I am thinking of redoing my home interior according to Feng shui. I am born in the year 1958. What would my be auspicious directions?

Q. My dining table is in the entrance hallway, between two rooms. How does this rate in Feng shui terms.? Also can you suggest ways of enhancing this situation with Feng shui ?

Q. My kitchen is very small and crowded. How can I improve it without breaking up any walls?

APPENDIX-B

THE CHINESE CALENDER AND
AUSPICIOUS/ELEMENTS & DIRECTIONS FOR YOU

The table suggests the ideal direction to orient your Home/Front Door, (For both Males and Females), Your Cabin in office in relation to the rest of the space or the Main Door with respect to the living room and the bedrooms.

YEAR	FROM	TO	BIRTH ELEMENT	ANIMAL SIGN	MALE	FEMALE
1914	26 Jan 1914	13 Feb 1915	Wood	Tiger	NE	SE
1915	14 Feb 1915	2 Feb 1916	Wood	Rabbit	N	NE
1916	3 Feb 1916	22 Jan 1917	Fire	Dragon	S	S
1917	23 Jan 1917	10 Feb 1918	Fire	Snake	NE	N
1918	11 Feb 1918	31 Jan 1919	Earth	Horse	SE	SW
1919	1 Feb 1919	19 Feb 1920	Earth	Ram	E	W
1920	20 Feb 1920	7 Feb 1921	Metal	Monkey	SW	NW
1921	8 Feb 1921	27 Jan 1922	Metal	Rooster	NW	SW
1922	28 Jan 1922	15 Feb 1923	Water	Dog	W	E

YEAR	FROM	TO	BIRTH ELEMENT	ANIMAL SIGN	MALE	FEMALE
1924	5 Feb. 1924	24 Jan 1925	Wood	Rat	N	NE
1925	25 Jan 1925	12 Feb 1926	Wood	Ox	S	S
1926	13 Feb 1926	1 Feb 1927	Fire	Tiger	NE	N
1927	2 Feb 1927	22 Jan 1928	Fire	Rabbit	SE	SW
1928	23 Jan 1928	9 Feb 1929	Earth	Dragon	E	W
1929	10 Feb 1929	29 Jan 1930	Earth	Snake	SW	NW
1930	30 Jan 1930	16 Feb 1931	Metal	Horse	NW	SW
1931	17 Feb 1931	15 Feb 1932	Metal	Ram	W	E
1932	6 Feb 1932	25 Jan 1933	Water	Monkey	NE	SE
1933	26 Jan 1933	13 Feb 1934	Water	Rooster	N	NE
1934	14 Feb 1934	3 Feb 1935	Wood	Dog	S	S
1935	4 Feb 1935	23 Jan 1936	Wood	Pig	NE	N
1936	24 Jan 1936	10 Feb 1937	Fire	Rat	SE	SW
1937	11 Feb 1937	30 Jan 1938	Fire	Ox	E	W
1938	31 Jan 1938	18 Feb 1939	Earth	Tiger	SW	NW
1939	19 Feb 1939	7 Feb 1940	Earth	Rabbit	NW	SW
1940	8 Feb 1940	26 Jan 1941	Metal	Dragon	W	E
1941	27 Jan 1941	14 Feb 1942	Metal	Snake	NE	SE
1942	15 Feb 1942	24 Feb 1943	Water	Horse	N	NE
1943	5 Feb 1943	24 Jan 1944	Water	Ram	S	S
1944	25 Jan 1944	12 Feb 1945	Wood	Monkey	NE	N
1945	13 Feb 1945	1 Feb 1946	Wood	Rooster	SE	SW
1946	2nd Feb 1946	21st Jan 1947	Fire	Dog	E	W
1947	22nd Jan 1947	9th Feb 1948	Fire	Pig	SW	NW
1948	10th Jan 1948	28th Jan 1949	Earth	Rat	NW	SW
1949	29th Feb 1949	16th Feb 1950	Earth	Ox	W	E

YEAR	FROM	TO	BIRTH ELEMENT	ANIMAL SIGN	MALE	FEMALE
1952	27th Jan 1952	13th Feb 1953	Water	Dragon	S	S
1953	14th Feb 1953	2nd Feb 1954	Water	Snake	NE	N
1954	3rd Feb 1954	23rd Jan 1955	Wood	Horse	SE	SW
1955	24th Jan 1955	11th Feb 1956	Wood	Ram	E	W
1956	12Feb 1956	30th Jan 1957	Fire	Monkey	SW	NW
1957	31st Jan 1957	17th Feb 1958	Fire	Rooster	NW	SW
1958	18th Feb 1958	7th Feb 1959	Earth	Dog	W	E
1959	8th Feb 1959	27th Jan 1960	Earth	Pig	NE	SE
1960	28th Jan 1960	14th Feb 1961	Metal	Rat	N	NE
1961	15th Feb 1961	4th Feb 1962	Metal	Ox	S	S
1962	5th Feb 1962	24th Jan 1963	Water	Tiger	NE	N
1963	25th Jan 1963	12thFeb 1964	Water	Rabbit	SE	SW
1964	13thFeb 1964	1st Feb 1965	Wood	Dragon	E	W
1965	2nd Feb 1965	20th Jan 1966	Wood	Snake	SW	NW
1966	21st Jan 1966	8th Feb 1967	Fire	Horse	NW	SW
1967	9th Feb 1967	29th Jan 1968	Fire	Ram	W	E
1968	30th Jan 1968	16th Feb 1969	Earth	Monkey	NE	SE
1969	17th Feb 1969	5th Feb 1970	Earth	Rooster	N	NE
1970	6th Feb 1970	26th Jan 1971	Metal	Dog	S	S
1971	27th Jan 1971	15th Feb 1972	Metal	Pig	NE	N
1972	16th Feb 1972	22nd Feb 1973	Water	Rat	SE	SW
1973	3rd Feb 1973	22nd Jan 1974	Water	Ox	E	W
1974	23rd Jan 1974	10th Feb 1975	Wood	Tiger	SW	NW
1975	11th Feb 1975	30th Jan 1976	Wood	Rabbit	NW	SW
1976	31st Jan 1976	17th Feb 1977	Fire	Dragon	W	E
1977	18th Feb 1977	6th Feb 1978	Fire	Snake	NE	SE

YEAR	FROM	TO	BIRTH ELEMENT	ANIMAL SIGN	MALE	FEMALE
1979	28th Jan 1979	15th Feb 1980	Earth	Ram	S	S
1980	16th Feb 1980	4th Feb 1981	Metal	Monkey	NE	N
1981	5th Feb 1981	24th Jan 1982	Metal	Rooster	SE	SW
1982	25th Jan 1982	12th Feb 1983	Water	Dog	E	W
1983	13th Feb 1983	1st Feb 1984	Water	Pig	SW	NW
1984	2nd Feb 1984	19th Feb 1985	Wood	Rat	NW	SW
1985	20th Feb 1985	8th Feb 1986	Wood	Ox	W	E
1986	9th Feb 1986	28th Jan 1987	Fire	Tiger	NE	SE
1987	29th Jan 1987	16th Feb 1988	Fire	Rabbit	N	NE
1988	17th Feb 1988	5th Feb 1989	Earth	Dragon	S	S
1989	6th Feb 1989	26th Jan 1990	Earth	Snake	NE	N
1990	27th Jan 1990	14th Feb 1991	Metal	Horse	SE	SW
1991	15th Feb 1991	3rd Feb 1992	Metal	Ram	E	W
1992	4th Feb 1992	22nd Jan 1993	Water	Monkey	SW	NW
1993	23rd Jan 1993	9th Feb 1994	Water	Rooster	NW	SW
1994	10th Feb 1994	30th Jan 1995	Wood	Dog	W	E
1995	31st Jan 1995	18th Feb 1996	Wood	Pig	NE	SE
1996	19th Feb 1996	7th Feb 1997	Fire	Rat	N	NE
1997	8th Feb 1997	27th Jan 1998	Fire	Ox	S	S
1998	28th Jan 1998	15th Feb 1999	Earth	Tiger	NE	N
1999	16th Feb 1999	4th Feb 2000	Earth	Rabbit	SE	SW
2000	5th Feb 2000	23rd Jan 2001	Metal	Dragon	E	W
2001	24th Jan 2001	11th Feb 2002	Metal	Snake	SW	NW
2002	12th Feb 2002	31st Jan 2003	Water	Horse	NW	SW
2003	1st Feb 2003	21st Jan 2004	Water	Ram	W	E

YEAR	FROM	TO	BIRTH ELEMENT	ANIMAL SIGN	MALE	FEMALE
2005	9th Feb 2005	28th Jan 2006	Wood	Rooster	N	NE
2006	29th Jan 2006	17th Feb 2007	Fire	Dog	S	S
2007	18th Feb 2007	6th Feb 2008	Fire	Pig	NE	N

There is, in addition a further categorization of people
into "Eastern Life" and "Western Life" persons.
There is an allied concept of *"Kua Numbers"*,
that indicates a personal number that represents
a very useful and detailed personal orientation guide.
There are 8 such numbers and associated guidelines.

ADDITIONAL INFORMATION

FORTHCOMING PUBLICATIONS BY THE SAME AUTHOR:
- **"MORE FENG SHUI ANSWERS"**-
With simple/ practical replies to a an exhaustive list of queries on
Feng shui for the work place (corporate, retail, industrial, institutional etc)
Includes pertinent tips for property evaluation
- **"THE ESSENTIAL FENG SHUI HANDBOOK"**-
Levels 1& 2,a set of books with lucid explanations/correlations of fundamental
Feng shui concepts and step- by step techniques for successful Feng shui implementation. A guided
tour through middle and advanced level techniques,
With diagrams, illustrations, case studies and check lists
- **"FENG SHUI TIPS FOR INTERIOR DESIGN"**-
Practical enhancements, Auspicious arrangements, Effective accessories.
Especially for persons somewhat familiar with Feng shui, looking for easy, usable design ideas for
enhancing their home and work place.
- **"FENG SHUI FOR THE MODERN SOUL"**- Revitalize Life & Space.
Comprehensive guidelines, for Space ordering, and Life enhancing through Feng shui for the
Millennium. Describes in great detail, manners of taking a real life Feng shui audit and reconciling all
the often-contradictory schools of thought
into a synergetic solution that is practicable too.
- **FENG SHUI * VAASTU SHASTRA**- Cosmic Guidelines for a Richer Life
Traditional Secrets for an Auspicious Built Environment.
An in-depth analysis of Feng shui with respect to the ancient Vedic subject-
Vaastu Shastra. A thorough comparison of both the arts
Aiming to endow readers with fresh and comprehensive insight,
Thus empowering educated choice.

BIBLIOGRAPHY

Birdsall, George, The Feng shui companion, (Destiny Books, Vermont,1997)

Brown, Simon, Principles of Feng shui, (Thorsons, London,1996)

Gordon, Rolf, Are you Sleeping in a Safe Place? (Dulwich Health Society, London, 1993)

Kingston, Karen, Creating Sacred Space with Feng shui,(Broadway Books, New York, 1997

Kwok, Man-Ho and O'Brien, Joanne, The Elements of Feng shui, (Element Books, Shaftesbury, 1991)

Lo, Raymond, Feng shui: The Pillars of Destiny : Understanding Your Fate and Fortune, (Time Editions, Singapore, 1995

Mair. H, Victor, Translation of Tao Te Ching-Lao Tzu, (Bantam Books, United States, Canada, 1990)

Reifler, Sam, I Ching-A New interpretation for Modern Times, (Bantam Books, United States, Canada, 1991)

Rossbach, Sarah, Interior Design with Feng shui, (Rider, London 1987)

Sandifer, Jon, Feng shui Journey,(Piatkus, London,1999)

Skinner, Stephen, Feng shui: The traditional oriental way to enhance your life,(Parragon, Great Britain, 1997)

Waring, Philippa, The Way of Feng shui: Harmony, Health, Wealth and Happiness, (Souvenir Press, Canada,1993)